THE OPERATOR DEVELOPMENT
PROGRAM „ODP"

Marcus Karl HAMAN, MSc

THE OPERATOR DEVELOPMENT
PROGRAM "ODP"

production management for managers

Bibliographic Information of the German National Library:

The German National Library lists this publication in the German National bibliography; detailed bibliographical data can be called up in the internet over http://dnb.dnb.de.

Illustration: HCA-consulting GmbH,
               CanStockPhoto
Translation: Prakash Chitale

Further collaborators: HCA-consulting GmbH

Production and Publishers: BoD–Books on Demand, Norderstedt

ISBN: 9783753423159

INTRODUCTION   8

OBJECTIVE OF THE WORKER DEVELOPMENT PROGRAM: 9
PURPOSE OF THE WORKER DEVELOPMENT PROGRAM: 10

DELIMITATION / GENERAL   11

CAREER PATHS   11
THE EXPERTS ORIENTATION   12
THE TRAINER AS MULTIPLICATOR   13
THE MANAGEMENT ORIENTATION (NOT IN CASE OF THE
AGILE ORGANIZATION STRUCTURE)   17
THE FLEXIBLE OR BROAD ORIENTATION   20
QUESTION CATALOGUE   22

ANALYSIS   23

THE EVALUATION & OVERVIEW   23
THE FLEXIBILLITY MATRIX   24
THE QUALIFICATION MATRIX   29
ORGANIZATION STRUCTURES   33
THE HIERARCHICAL ORGANIZATION STRUCTURE   34
THE TEAM-ORIENTED ORGANIZATION STRUCTURE   36
THE AGILE ORGANIZATION STRUCTURE   37
QUESTIONNAIRE   43
THE JOB DESCRIPTION   44
THE JOB TICKETS   45
THE WORKPLACE DESCRIPTION   47
QUESTIONNAIRE   50
PROCESSES & CORE PROCESSES   51

THE STANDARDIZED WORKSHEET (SOS)   **54**
QUESTIONNAIRE   **57**

CONCEPTION   **58**

THE STRATEGY   **60**
POTENTIALS   **62**
FURTHER DEVELOPMENT   **63**
PROMOTE & DEMAND   **64**
QUESTIONNAIRE   **66**
THE AGILE APPROACH   **67**
QUESTIONNAIRE   **73**
COMMITMENT   **74**
QUESTIONNAIRE   **77**
THE TRAINING PROCESS   **78**
QUESTIONNAIRE   **85**
INTERNAL TRAINERS & EXTERNAL TRAINERS   **86**
THE CERTIFICATION   **88**
THE DIFFERENT KNOWLEDGE LEVELS   **93**
KNOWLEDGE LEVEL 1 – BASIC KNOWLEDGE   96
KNOWLEDGE LEVEL 2 – EXTENDED KNOWLEDGE   98
KNOWLEDGE LEVEL 3 – EXPERT LEVEL   100
QUESTIONNAIRE   **102**
TRAINING PROGRAM KNOWLEDGE LEVEL 1   **103**
KNOWLEDGE LEVEL BASIC TRAINING MODULE 1 -
KNOWING / MEASURING / PRODUCT   105
KNOWLEDGE LEVEL BASIC TRAINING MODULE 2 –
CLEANING & INSPECTION   111
KNOWLEDGE LEVEL BASIC TRAINING MODULE 3 –
OPERATE   116

KNOWLEDGE LEVEL BASIC TRAINING - MODULE 4 -
PERFORM   123
SALARY STRUCTURE   **126**
POSSIBILITIES OF REMUNERATION TO THE EMPLOYEE WITH THE
HELP OF THE ODP: 127
QUESTIONNAIRE   **134**

IMPLEMENTATION   **135**

FAILED RECIPES   **139**
REVIEW   **141**
TO CELEBRATE THE FIRST SUCCESSES   **143**
SETBACKS   **144**

ABBREVIATIONS   **146**

FURTHER BOOKS BY MARCUS KARL HAMAN   **148**

NOTES   **149**

NOTES   **150**

NOTES   **151**

An undertaking should be considered like a living organism. In order to exist, each „form of life" must develop itself further. May this be by experiencing and collecting of experience or through specific transfer of knowledge.

The most effective approach to improve the organization is certainly the training of the people or employees, who ensure the core business. In the example of a production plant, these are the workers or production employees.

However, the difficulty is to implement the transfer of knowledge in a regulated and controlled or structured manner. Similarly subjects like wage structure and function allowances as well as the desire of the undertaking to make progress are always present. May this be professional, personal, methodical or hierarchical.

With limited availability of personnel in the market, training programs are a decision criterion to decide for the one or the other undertaking. Training programs should be accessible to every employee, or when considered further, they should be a wish or demand of the management to accompany the program actively and implement it.

Similarly, the career path is an important component in the training management of a production unit.

There is not only the management or leadership career. Also, the expert or specialist career is an attractive career path for the employee, when this is correspondingly communicated and lived.

Objective of the worker development program:

To establish a standardized training and development management, the objective of which is to ensure the success of the undertaking. Through an all-encompassing further development of the individual employees, considerable improvements are achieved in the areas of work safety, quality and productivity, which then reflect in the field of costs. Only when the employees know their tasks, responsibilities and objectives, a targeted focusing on the objectives of the undertaking and their achievement is enabled.

The purpose lies in the fact that the market is serviced at optimum cost, as far as possible without waste, or justice is done to the requirements of the market. Especially the availability of or the delivery periods of products are an important success factor, which can be ensured only on a broad level. Market leadership can be achieved only then, when the entire organization knows as to which functions and responsibilities every individual has.

„The enabling must come before setting up the objective and it should be experienced from the 1st day."

CAREER PATHS

There are essentially 3 (+1) career paths within production organization at the worker level, which acts in the team-oriented organization structure:

1. The flexible or broad orientation
2. The management orientation &
3. The experts orientation and
   3.1. The Trainer as Multiplicator (Experts orientation)

Each of these orientations has the same importance and the same significance for the undertaking. The positions and task areas are connected with each other and dependent on each other. Excepted from this is the career path of the management personnel in agile organization structures.

The expert orientation envisages that an employee acquires a very deep knowledge in a particular process. This can be achieved only with great difficulty over several processes, since the depth of knowledge is very high and in order to stay up to date, the employee must continuously confront himself with the subject. For the expert it is important to develop himself further steadily and sustainably. If an expert possesses the capability to be able to give his expertise further, then the expert should be trained to become a trainer. Through the knowledge transfer by an own employee, a multiplicator is established in an undertaking, who promotes other employees and thus the entire organization experiences a value addition, which comes from within the organization.

The career path Expert is the pre-requisite for the Trainer Status. However, not every expert can also provide knowledge and therefore he also cannot carry out the function as trainer. For the success of this role, it is necessary to have the will and the competence to be able to share his/her knowledge. Many experts live in the world, having to protect their knowledge, so that they cannot be substituted and show a unique position characteristic within the organization without being affected. Similarly, many are driven by the compulsion of having to achieve a special position in the undertaking in order to consolidate their status, which actually does not exist and shall never exist, so far as the management is not weak and thinks that it is dependent upon experts. Because one thing is quite clear:

„Every man and woman in an organization can be substituted and the man on the machine cannot be substituted as quickly as the manager, for whom the company is responsible. "

Especially it is the will to pass on the knowledge acquired over several years which

13

makes up the transformation of the expert into the trainer.

The competence is already a separate aspect, because, as already remarked above, not every expert can convey knowledge. There are indeed instruction programs and trainings to learn this, however, more than this is necessary. The basis of this capability as also the recognition that passing on of knowledge represents a considerable further development of the entire organization and thus strengthens the competitiveness or secures the jobs must be promoted or supported by the management. No expert shall be questioned or substituted because he passes on knowledge. On the contrary, an expert, who is ready to pass on his knowledge to the organization, is one of the most valuable employees in the undertaking. Not as a special case and not as irreplaceable, however with respect and recognition of his performance and his contribution, which he is ready to perform for the undertaking.

The schooling of experts to trainers should be done in a previously compiled training program. The Training to Trainer should perhaps be considered externally. The external trainings have for instance an independent manner to convey knowledge. The would-be trainers have the possibility in a "protected space" to ask free questions, to carry out role-plays and to conduct exchange of experience with other participants, without this in any way coming up within the own organization, in which the future trainer is active. Not that this would be undertaken, however, the internal fear is always present that everyone hears everything or notices it. Therefore, during internal programs many employees hold themselves back, since they are worried to be noticed negatively and this has an effect at a later time. What does not take place in most of the organizations, however, the thought of safety to endanger one's working place in some way or the other is present in many heads, whether confessed or not. In case of an external event, to a certain degree, this is not the case, however, the trainer himself decides this with his action.

The external trainer takes over the conveyance of the competence for knowledge transfer. This is possible, since this knowledge represents a general knowledge. It does not require any special knowledge of the actual organization. Merely the structure of the undertaking should be a part of this training so that the future trainer can appropriately react to

any problems or does not enter into the situations totally unprepared.

THE MANAGEMENT ORIENTATION (Not in case of the agile organization structure)

The management orientation is by far the most well-known possibility of further development. In the undertaking, in which possibilities are organized hierarchically or team oriented. Since agile organization structures do not know any management levels, the management orientation is dropped.

The classic case for the employee career for hierarchical and team-oriented organizations straightly. Everyone wants to be 'the boss' and let others work. This at least is the opinion

of many, who, however, never had a leadership responsibility. The difference between a superior and a management person cannot be greater than this. The manager of a group is indeed determined and ‚made available ‚, as against which a leading person has the responsibility of leadership within a team and through competences and performance exercises the position. A manager accompanies and acts as coach with social competence, however, also with strength of implementation on the team for which he is responsible.

This book does not deal with management im-

TEAMMEMBER WITH RESPONSIBILITY

plementation. Whereby it should however be mentioned that just like a operator development program (ODP), there is also a management development program, called in short MDP, in the team-oriented and the hierarchical organization structure, which should be implemented in all productive undertakings. In case of agile organization structures the MDP is absent, since in the agile organization structure there are no managing personnel or deploys no managing personnel.

And one thing should still be mentioned:

„When the management is weak, as weak is the team itself. "

A not so common orientation or the possibility of further development of employees within an organization is offered by the flexible or also broad orientation. If the expert orientation goes down very much, then the competence of an employee, which the broad orientation has selected, is distributed to several working places, however, not to such a depth as that of an expert. This is not so much about detailed process knowledge, much rather it is the flexibility of the employee with reference to operating several machines, systems or workplaces.

Both the experts as also the broad, flexible orientation is significant for the success of the undertaking.

Important for the success of the undertaking is also the distribution between experts and broadly divided employees. Alone the experts are not target-oriented for a production undertaking. As against this the organization can very well survive without experts. The organization must only ensure, that the non-available competences of the individual processes are externally available. However, this is not always available at call and if at all, then certainly at a very high cost. A not insignificant side effect is then the resulting reaction period and the related downtimes of the individual systems and machines.

Which career paths are there on the Worker Level?

What is the difference between Expert and Trainer?

Which of these career paths is the most important one in the organization?

Wherein lies the difference between the flexible and the expert orientation?

Which 2 development programs are there in the organization?

THE EVALUATION & OVERVIEW

An important step to improve oneself is the evaluation of the competences of the individual employees. On the one hand, in order to see which level of knowledge and capability the individual employees show, and on the other hand to recognize, where their deficiency of knowledge and capability is. These should be continuously and sustainably improved or developed further. Only through the continuous further development and involvement of each individual employee the undertaking can grow to a learning organization.

There are two areas to carry out an evaluation. The area Flexibility and the area Knowledge & Training. Both the areas are equally important for the undertaking. Only being flexibly usable is simply too little. In order to survive in the market as a successful undertaking, it is not sufficient to employ employees, who can be used at several workplaces. Employees should also possess the professional, personal and methodical capabilities, which are essential for the success of the organization. These are held in a qualification matrix and evaluated or regularly questioned.

THE FLEXIBILLITY MATRIX

The flexibility matrix as well as the qualification matrix consists of two areas.
In the flexibility matrix in the vertical column all the employees are listed and in the horizontal level all the workplaces. In the qualification matrix in the horizontal level the subjects and trainings are listed in place of the workplaces. In the flexibility matrix it is important to list here all process sections, since otherwise some competences are not considered, however, they are important for the success and for the further development.
A process section is for instance a workplace, a machine, a plant, manual working places or a post-processing station. Similarly test stations or store places or buffer areas etc. represent a process section. An example should represent this a little simplified.

Employee	Workplace I	Workplace II	Workplace X
Hr. May			

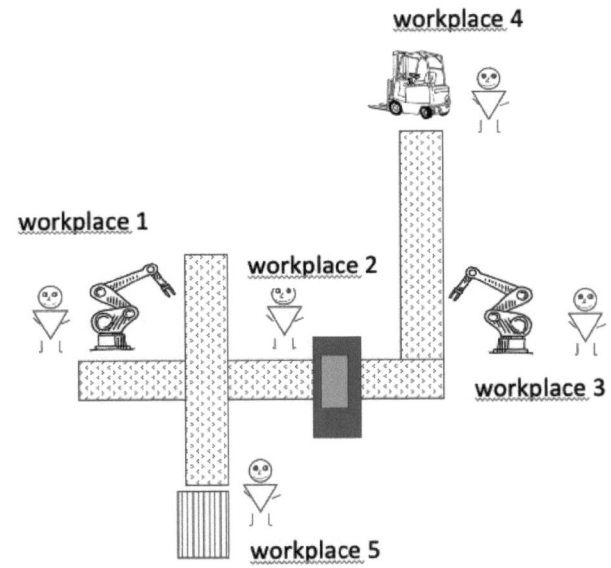

Each of the employees, shown here in the picture, works at a process section or workplace. All these workplaces must be learnt, the employees must be enabled. This is implemented in classical fashion in many undertakings in the form of a „learning by doing" training strategy. On entry the employees are exposed to a workplace in the new firm and in many instances also more or less left alone after a very short training period. No standards at the workplace like standardized worksheets and process descriptions, are not an exception. This in turn has a negative effect not only on the quality but also on the productivity.

The new employee shall certainly pose questions during the training. After the training he may pose questions once or twice, however, after that he shall rather hold himself back and since he sees his workplace endangered, he would rather keep quiet about errors, which he causes due to the lack of experience and knowledge. The fault shall then be very quickly found with the new employee, however, if the situation is observed with objective distance, then the cause of error is clearly visible. The management has fully and totally failed. Failed due to the fact that no standards, no structured and planned transfer of knowledge was made available or conveyed to the new employee.

The difference between the classical and the structured form is a time-related difference which reflects itself in the duration. If a structured training lasts some 2 months, then the training of the new employee, on a non-standardized workplace with no structured transfer of knowledge would last minimum 4-6 months. And the sustainability must also be questioned.

A well-trained employee not only brings more performance at a faster pace, but he shall also provide his performance at the place of work also with greater motivation. The reason for this simply is that he feels himself safe dealing with his functions. With self-assurance the new employee can achieve success due to the fact that he achieves his goals being more stress-free and more motivated and thus can make a substantial contribution to the success of the undertaking. He shall also be integrated faster in the team, since he can make his contribution in the team.

The flexibility matrix is divided in to 4 knowledge levels with every workplace. The first knowledge level means that the employee has reached BASIC knowledge level. The second knowledge level reflects the EXPANDED knowledge area. The third level shows that the employee is an EXPERT on the said workplace and the fourth knowledge level identifies the employee as TRAINER at the said workplace.

Thus, it is ensured that there is a clear and structured overview over the knowledge level and competence of every individual employee in connection with the individual workplaces. Managers can then adopt preventive measures in order to reduce the knowledge gaps or to eliminate them.

In the flexibility matrix the knowledge levels are represented or shown as follows:

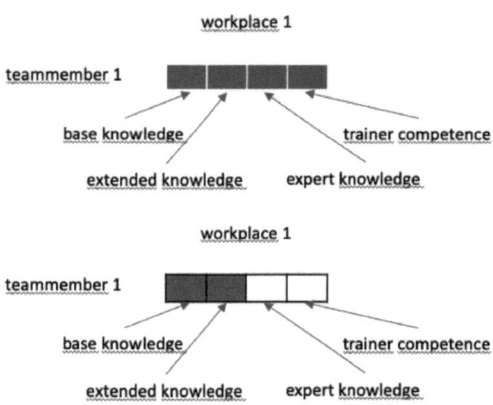

teammember 1 has at workplace 1 extended knowledge

As against this the qualification matrix has the task to consider the training side of the individual employee. If the Flex Matrix is focused on processes, the quality matrix deals with the knowledge level for the topics methods, systems, basic trainings and the professional training.

Just like the flex matrix, also in this case there are 4 knowledge levels, which are reflected for each employee. The first knowledge level shows that the employee shows BASIC knowledge of a subject. One subject is for instance the method „7 types of waste". Here the employee has a basic knowledge of this subject. He has learnt the topic in theoretical lessons and has within the framework of this training got acquainted with a practical access in the form of an example on the shopfloor. The second knowledge level, EXTENDED KNOWLEDGE, is reached by the employee through a further theoretical portion and the knowledge as to how the method is used in practice. He has likewise implemented his first project for the topic 7 types of wastage and can apply this in daily use.

The employee reaches the third knowledge level, EXPERT, when he has the sound knowledge about the subject and has executed at least 10 projects in his own responsibility and when the results are verifiable in a sustained manner. The fourth and last knowledge level, TRAINER, can be reached by the employee, when the employee, besides his competence as expert, also displays the capability of knowledge transfer.

„Not every expert can and would like to pass on knowledge further. "

Also, in the qualification matrix the knowledge gaps and risks of the team are displayed, which then can be used by the respective leader for closing these and to develop his team further sustainably and continuously.

When the flexibility and qualification matrix per team are considered, immediately the knowledge and competence gaps become visible. From this in turn the training and development potentials on the team and employee level are worked out, then worked out in a personal development plan and prepared for implementation. It is then the responsibility of the organization to get hold of this ball and to promote the undertaking with respect to knowledge technology and also to make demands on it.

The competences of the Flex matrix and of the qualification matrix are measured in a form/data sheet, which is designed on the team level and it is communicated by posting at Team Info Center, a Team board / Team blackboard, which are installed in team area and are accessible to all.

On the form, the knowledge level or the competence is clearly visible through the sub-division in 4 stages. Thus, not only the team but also the employee or the managers immediately become conscious, as to where the respective employee or also the team shows weaknesses. Countermeasures are then possible on fair basis in a very specific manner.

In the following example an extract of an evaluation from a flexibility matrix is illustrated.

The team member 1 has an extended knowledge regarding the method "7 type of waste".

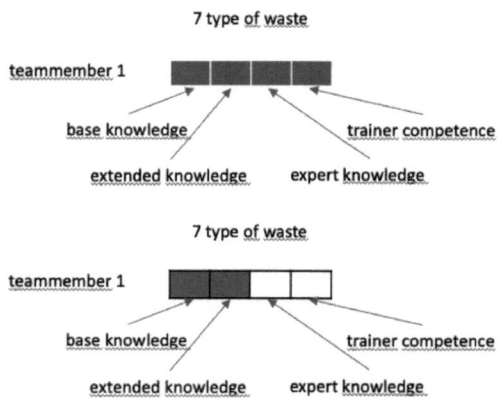

teammember 1 has extended knowledge regarding „7 type of waste"

The right organization structure is very important for the success of the undertaking. To a great extent the organization structure is defined through the culture of the undertaking. This shape and aligns the entire organization and has a direct influence on the success. Culture of an undertaking must always be lived exemplarily, „TOP – DOWN", by the Top Management, in order to establish this effectively within the organization and to achieve the desired success. An organization structure lives from the culture which prevails in the undertaking. And thus, this should be selected carefully and lived or claimed consistently.

There are the most diverse organization structures in the production environment. The strictly hierarchical, the team-oriented or the agile structure. The last named is a rather new, already somewhat revolutionary approach, which correspondingly differs from the other organization structures.

There is however every kind of mutation or adjusted structures and mixed forms. Whichever is selected, it should be authentically lived. An organization structure, which is implemented halfheartedly or for the sake of alibi, shall not function on the one hand and cause more damage than being useful on the other hand.

The most frequently used form of the organization structure in the last years is the team-oriented organization structure. This is used or practiced in very consistent form in the automobile industry and the automobile supplier industry. The strictly hierarchical structure and company structure is rather found in the family or owner managed undertakings.

The hierarchical organization structure

One of the oldest organization forms is that of the hierarchical ones. This type of organization structure is very well spread in the governmental organizations as for instance in the military field or the administration or in other organizations. However, also in many family units and owner managed units this form of organization is maintained and practiced.

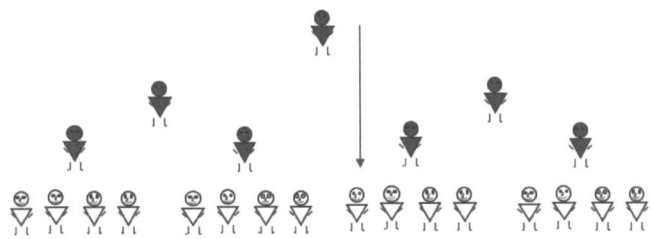

In this form of organization that is implemented, what and how the ‚boss‘ would like to have it. It resembles more to an issue of command, where thinking along and getting involved do not come under the order of the day and it is considered rather as very critical. In many organizations this perhaps makes sense, however, not in a production organization aligned to the market, which has the objective to generate profit and which claims to be a further developing organization. As a rule this type of organization functions in many units in such a way that one is ‚servant‘ for those above, for the colleagues at the same level he is the „irrelevant one“ and for those below he is the „ruler“ in the theater of the undertaking. In every show, taking place every day, commands are issued and stubbornly implemented, without wasting a single spark of personal participation of thinking along.

Starting from an automobile industry and other industries stuck in crisis the Team for Organization was developed and implemented. From the necessity to save costs. A wise man proposed the theory that many heads would have more ideas that only a single one. What revolutionary thinking – from the present-day view, however, at that time it was really a kind of revolution and required a management, which was ready to start the rethinking process. The success made the management right, because to use the unused potentials in order to act more successfully is a sensible attitude, which can bring forward the undertaking. Teams were formed and everyone was asked to make his contribution. Premia for good ideas which would bring the undertaking further were paid out to the employees and the motivation was essentially raised with the integration of all employees in the decision processes. And with the motivation of the employees to improve and to change something, the successes set in. Teams led by managers created the basis within the organization and objectives were 'achieved' Top – Down. In many instances up to the employee level.

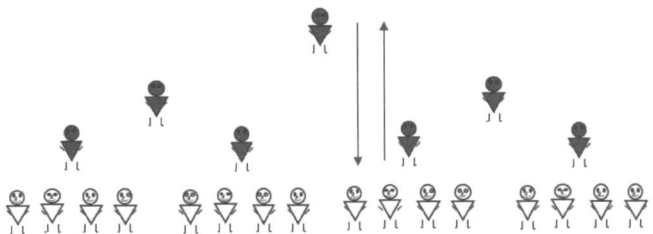

The agile Organization structure

New periods and needs bring new forms of organization structures in undertakings. The need is a good motivator for a management to generate high profits and it stands under pressure to ensure their bonus or to make the undertaking more successful and generate more profit. The agile organization form is a possibility to shape the undertaking still slimmer and thus more profitable.

As a matter of fact, the agile form of organization puts to test the courage for modification within the management. It requires more than only the decision to try it. It shall have to give a re-thinking process within the entire team, in order to implement the conversion successfully. During this, as also during every other change, it is important to experience and claim the new culture. However, also to

promote it and to convey it clearly and precisely in the background.

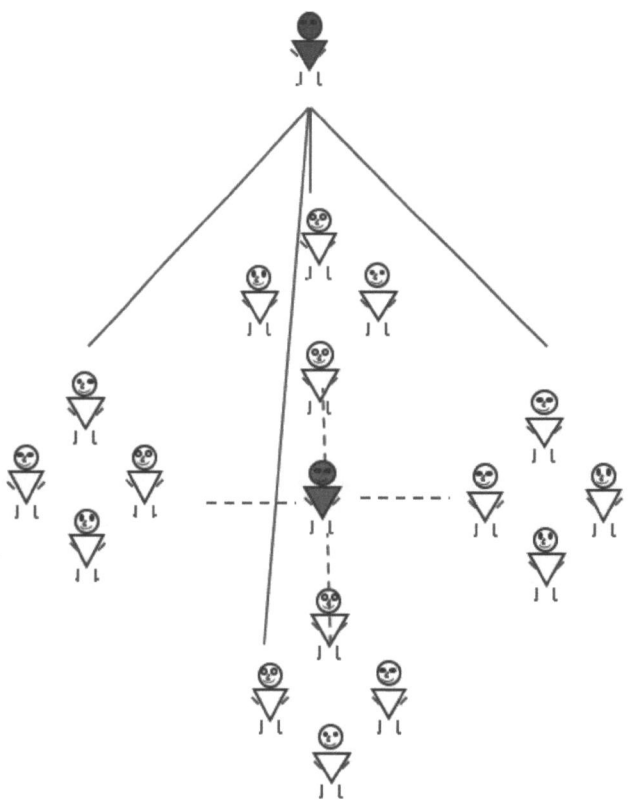

The agile form of organization can survive
only then, when it was also understood within
the organization. A lot of enlightenment and
training or understanding shall be the order of

the day of the so-called „Coaches", because one searches in vain for managers within an agile organization. This is also the greatest difference and point of discussion, which stands in the area of change, should the Top Management decide in favor of implementing this form of organization. How does an agile organization without managers function and who provides the objectives or who says how it goes?

These and other questions raise themselves immediately, when it is necessary to imagine a professional habitat without managers. This already borders on anarchy, as „hardcore" critics say. Everyone can rule and behave as he likes!

Naturally it is not so. The difference lies in the fact that all team members jointly introduce a decision above their area of responsibility. All on the same level. And should there be contradictory aspects or/and disagreements then the supervisor is on the spot as mediator or moderator and he advises rightly without hierarchical intervention. Through his knowledge and experience he can stand by the side of the teams, because he is not responsible only for one team. The supervisor „coached" up to 7 teams. The objective within the team is implemented and passed by the team itself. The team sets up its goals for itself, which it would like to reach. And this is also one of the strengths in this system. When objectives are set up by the team itself, then the team members also stand behind them and shall do a lot for that to reach the objectives or to exceed them. It can be compared with a video game, which continuously motivates us subconsciously to reach the next level, or to set up the next record. From the own motivation and not through stipulation of a manager or of the management. Self-determination is the highest form of integration of all the employees. The main objective is prescribed by a board or a chief executive, however not the team objectives.

Not everything is as simple as it sounds. Especially at the beginning many questions, misunderstandings, different interpretations of the objectives and many other topics shall come up, which should be counteracted with a lot of training, schooling, explanation and care. There are risks hiding behind these, however, the so-called failure recipes can help in the background to prepare oneself for eventualities. Failure recipes contain a single question, which the team or the management work out or answer:

„What we must do so that it does not function or so that we are not successful? ".

This type of questioning is important in order also to consider the „negative" view. As a rule, the moderator is overwhelmed by the participants or almost killed by reasons as to why something does not function. And this is well so, because for every point observed also a countermeasure must be formulated, which has the objective to prevent the "case".

For instance, the interaction between the individual teams, which should not be greater than up to 9 persons, is very important. In case of a process chain, which acts coherently, and which includes several teams, these teams must attune with each other. Here the caretaker is very much required to ensure the objectivity and to explain transparently the relationship between customer and supplier, which acquires great importance. Because when a team has set the objective, which means 40 components in one hour, however the successor process of the next team expects an objective of 60 components in an hour, then conflict potentials are presented, which are taken on record by the supervisor and which must be brought closer to both the teams with arguments and explanation.

Here the agile system finds its limits. When the teams do not have the desire to tread this path openly, this organization shall fail. The compilation of the individual teams shall thus be an important milestone in the implementation of the agile organization structure, which fact requires special attention.

- Which organization structures are essentially there?

- Which differences are characteristic between the individual organization structures?

- What is the advantage of the agile organization structure?

- Wherein lies the risk in case of the agile organization structure?

- Normally, where is the hierarchical organization structure used and why?

- Which advantages does the team-oriented organization structure have vis-a-vis the hierarchical one?

The Job description, in German called activity description, is happily kept very general, since otherwise from the employer side there can be a restriction of the extensibility of the functions given to the employee. In the Production department it is however necessary to record everything clearly and precisely in writing. The more clearly described are the functions, also called role & responsibility, the clearer is also the view of the employee. The employee then knows the demands or the expectations of the management from him and can deal with them. One possibility of converting this in a very concrete and transparent form are the production handbooks, also called Job Ticket. These Job Tickets are prepared for every level and they represent the basis of a fair measurability of the employee.

The Job Tickets, also called employee hand-books, are detailed descriptions of the individual roles and responsibilities of the individual production levels, as for instance for the employee, the team leader, or the production manager. In the agile organization structure similarly handbooks are used, however, the management levels are taken from the grid.

Die Handbooks are divided in the following areas:

- Work safety & environment
- Quality
- Productivity / Delivery capacity
- Costs
- Stocks
- Organization development

The described functions and responsibilities give a clear agenda for the respective employee. Only when an employee knows the expectations of the organization, he can do justice to this claim of the organization. On the other hand, during the production of these handbooks, the organization deals with the demands that it makes from the employees or on which agendas work must be carried out within the organization in order to implement the ambitious objectives of the undertaking.

It is quite a great effort, with which the organization burdens itself in developing the handbooks, however in the medium and the long term the works pays off in multiples and with consistent implementation, which includes the setting of example by the management, the results shall be more and more efficient and effective, comprehensible and transparent.

The handbooks are matched to the respective level in the production department, however, provided with a „red thread", which reaches from the uppermost level to the worker level. In other words, the functions and responsibilities must be "broken down" more and more. The functions shall remain more or less the same between the levels, however, the responsibility of a production manager is certainly different than the responsibilities of the worker on the machine.

A workplace description has the following functions:

- Transparent representation of all the processes at the respective workplace
- Safety specifications and special applications regarding the subject work safety and environment
- Quality-related aspects and measurement methods or intervals
- Change of tools
- Conversion steps / Processes
- Specified periods
- Switching on and off of the machine/ system (if present)
- Manufacturing processes at the workplace
- Tools and their application
- Lock out / Knock out / Take out
- Layout of the workplace
- Cleaning and inspection documents
- Etc.

The presentation should be very easy to understand however self-explanatory. A massive effort, however, the result or rather the error percentage substantially better than without and thus the costs or the manufacturing costs become lower. And in many instances, these (costs) decide about the possibility of surviving in the market or not.

The workplace description is accessible to the worker at any time and can, on the one hand, be used as information, however also as reference work and learning material.

In the normal case the workplace description is divided in the following topics:

- Work safety and environment
- Quality &
- Productivity / Delivery capability

In the area Work Safety and Environment forms like Layout, lock out (switching on and off of the plant), Take out (securing of the machine during or for maintenance, inspection or repair work), hints regarding hazardous materials and their handling, waste separation etc. are kept ready for the employee.
For Quality and Productivity these are self-explanatory and step-by-step explained documents, in order to prevent mistakes or in order to ensure information as for instance guide for measuring quality or change of tools. A

pictorial documentation with clear instructions is a part of an excellent job description.

- What is the difference between a Job description and a Job Ticket?

- What is a workplace description?

- Which strength does a workplace description show?

- Which standardized work sheets should hang at a place of work and should be accessible to the employee at any time?

Processes are often not understood by the team, since these are not tangible. Something not real, withdrawn, with which only the management deals, if at all. As a rule, processes do not interest the team. There are more important things to be done on the Shopfloor (Production area).

Far from it, but the knowledge of the employee level comes only with explanation and training of the employees in this subject. Processes are potentials, which can be continuously improved, in so far as these are previously conveyed and were especially made measurable.

The difference between core processes and processes in general can be actually easily explained. A core business contains all the processes, which earn profit for the undertaking. All other processes are not core processes. As example, a production undertaking produces metal pins and delivers these as commissioned work to the customer. The process with which the undertaking generates profit is the production process. Herein thus is the core competence, i.e., the knowledge of the company to fabricate these pins. This process is thus the core process of this organization. All other processes are either management processes or support processes, also called supporting processes. A further difference is for instance that core processes, in contrast to all other processes, are never outsourced, since these processes (core processes) indeed earn profit, i.e. represent a „Profit Center" and the other processes cause costs and thus represent the so called „Cost Center".

When the processes, which are clearly documented in the environment of the affected employees, these can also be referred to as schooling and training documents. After the training they are also used as reference work. The pre-condition for this is that they are also maintained, that is matched in case of changes and the organization is informed about the modification. When an organization has recognized to use the advantages of a transparent process landscape and when this life, it will experience a further development thrust and thus a clear advantage vis-a-vis the competitor. The advantages for the organization are obvious. These are for instance the following:

- Training phases are substantially shortened
- A certification as per ISO is considerably simplified
- SOX subject is substantially simplified
- Avoiding of errors is visible
- Wastages are considerably reduced
- Saving potentials become easily visible
- Optimization of the individual processes/ Procedures are simplified
- Etc.

It is not an insignificant effort to document the processes clearly and to keep them up to date, however, the advantages from this work outweigh considerably the expenses. Process documentations and report systems of all departments (especially in finance and purchase etc. departments) are obligatory for larger undertakings and especially for undertakings which are quoted on a stock market in the USA.

(SOX - The Sarbanes-Oxley Act of 2002, is a US-Federal Law, which as a reaction to the balance sheet scandals of companies like Enron or WorldCom should improve the reliability of the reporting system of undertakings, which are using the public capital market of USA). (Source WIKIPEDIA 08/2019)

The standardized worksheet is the basis of a very efficient incorporation of new employees as also a securing for comprehensible results like quality and productivity. Similarly work safety aspects are kept very well in focus with that. The highest priority should be on work safety.

The standardized worksheet, in so far as this is practiced or adhered to, regulates the sequence of the individual process steps. Similarly, the measurement and control of the processes.

With a good development the standardized worksheet serves both as training document as well as reference work for the employee. The important thing is that the employee can read at any time all the specifications and work steps, without having to ask questions to anyone. This is essential, because especially new employees enquire perhaps 1-3 times, should something not be clear, however, from the third time onwards, should something not be clear, the employees would rather not ask any more, since in many instances they fear that they would be considered as incompetent and incapable of learning and thus see their workplace in the undertaking being endangered. Therefore, many employees keep quiet about errors and try to cover this also or hide them, should it deal with production components.

An example from practice:

A new employee was trained on a workplace. It was an automated workplace with a plant. Since there were no standardized documents at the machine, the training was carried out directly at the machine in verbal form. The team leader had also reached his bearable stress level with the daily tasks and could not really bother about the new employee. This one indeed asked question repeatedly, however, not any more after a few times. Errors happened and due to fear of losing the new workplace, he hid the faulty components. One year later, during the exchange of the line, numerous fabrication parts were found in the surroundings of the plant. In the inner area of the construction columns, in the floor of the cabinets, under the machine, etc.

On the one hand the employee is responsible to report, when he does not know what to do, however, it also lies under the responsibility of the management to undertake everything, that the POKA YOKE approach (POKA YOKE comes from Japanese and roughly means „make it right from the start and prevent errors from the beginning") is implemented as culture and holds. If standardized worksheets were present at the workplace, then the employee would have been able to read without losing "his face", or without endangering his workplace or being considered as incompetent to learn.

What are core processes?

How do core processes differ from other processes?

What should not be done with core processes?

What are SOSs (standardized worksheets) used for?

Which purpose do the SOSs have?

Which risk threatens when no SOSs are present at the workplace?

After the actual analyses phase follows the conception phase, also called SPECIFIED conception phase. The name is program in this section. In the specified conception phase, everything is planned to the smallest detail. Not only the WHAT, much rather the WHO, HOW and WHEN, are very strongly pushed into the focus here. The better is the planning, the more implementation successes will be there. The course plan of the organization for the implementation of the Worker Development Program.

It is urgently advised to take time for this, because later the planning details become very tedious, requiring a great amount of time and resources, and especially these topics act as partly de-motivating and frustrating for the team.

With the help of plans for measures and actions, in whatever form these may be, the employees can always and at any time read as to where the organization stands at this point and which points are still open. Thus, all the employees can pull on the same "rope" and support the project fully. It is recommended to make the action plans easily accessible within the organization, since otherwise the information would not penetrate 100% to the employee level. The so-called works and team boards, which hang not only on the shopfloor but also in the office area, are very good points of communication, which can easily and understandably transport the accessible information to the team, when they are also used for this purpose and regularly attended to.

An excellent strategy landscape is half the compensation on the stony path to success. The development of a strategy or of a strategy landscape with several strategies is a significant step to success or failure. A strategy should hold on and show validity for at least 1-3 years. Also, in a fast-paced period, in which we all find ourselves today, it is important to transport continuity and peace in the organization. Only when all the employees of the undertaking know the objectives and what should be achieved, then all can work on it and focus on it, irrespective of the fact, whether it is a team-oriented or an agile organization structure.

Finding a strategy is an important process and should not be dealt with quickly. The strategies are the path for the fulfillment of the mission statement of the respective organization. Therefore, all the employees must stand behind them. In order to be able to stand behind the strategies, it would be clever to include the employees in the formation process, or at least to keep them informed at the latest information level – pro-actively by the management.

From the specifications of the Top Management, the superior objectives are noted and communicated to the team. From these specifications it is necessary to work out strategies for the fulfillment of these superior objectives. The starting point is not only the results achieved in the current year. It will be a more or less large stew of ideas, results and experience, which the strategy court makes. And it is always better to work out less strategies than too many. Because the team must be able to implement these with the available resources. Less strategies, when they are consistently implemented, more effective and more profitable for the undertaking.

As a rule, about 5 strategies are worked out and implemented.

There are a large number of books, which describe and prepare the subject unused potentials within an organization. And in spite of this, there are still numerous undertakings, which do without using the potentials of the own team for the success of the undertaking. Nobody knows the machine or the workplace better than the employee, who works 8 hours per day with it. This is naturally also valid for every other workplace in other fields, whether operated with machines or manually.

It is quite in order and sometimes also very useful to fetch external views and experience in the organization, or to purchase the same, however, the potentials of the own team should be at least also referred to, in order to promote the continuous improvement process.

The further development of the total organization should stand quite at the top on the list on every agenda of an undertaking. Pre-requisite for this is that the organization is intending a long-term survival scenario, as also continuous increase in profit.

With further development not only the training of the individual employees is meant. Although this represents one of the largest items on the purchase slip of the management, there are several areas of further development, which the undertaking shall meet on the stony path of continuous improvement.

The ODP forms the base, that is, the broadest front in the undertaking. To make the mass of people capable and to distribute the knowledge to many is a significant step to success. Through the worker development program, the further development for the entire organization is brought to a higher level. The worker development program can also be referred to for administrative departments as template, naturally with a different content.

Potentials of improvement come into light under this consideration, which cannot be more profitable.

The promoting and demanding are important components of the continuous further development. Without promoting the employees and without making demands on them to participate proactively in the further development process of the undertaking, a further development shall not be possible. A motivating environment must be created, wherein the employees can participate in positive happenings. The knowledge of the employees about a positive development of the undertaking has a positive effect also for the employee himself and is essential and should not be underestimated. A „WIN WIN" situation is the best kind to achieve or realize progress.

In a team-oriented structural form of the undertaking all the managers are required especially to drive forward this topic. However, not with hierarchical management methods like ordering, monitoring and showing action.

As against this the motivation factors in an agile structure form must create a greater motivating environment, which encourages the employees to develop themselves further and to improve themselves continuously. Naturally here also the role of the companion /advisor assumes a special importance. To convince with arguments and to show, what advantage is there to devote thoughts to the CIP (continuous improvement process), this shall be a profitable strategy and it leads in many instances clearly to success.

- What are the main functions in the conception phase?

- What is a strategy?

- How long is a strategy valid?

- Where are potentials available in an undertaking?

- How can potentials be implemented?

- How are potentials promoted in an organization?

- For what purpose is a further development aspired in an undertaking?

- How should a further development take place?

- What is the difference between promoting and demanding?

- Who should be promoted and simultaneously subjected to demand in an undertaking?

The agile approach was already briefly referred to in an earlier chapter. However, since it deals with a new approach, the agile approach deserves a new consideration.

A rather new and in many production organizations revolutionary approach is the agile one. However, what does the "agile" approach mean? And what has this to do with the undertaking culture of an organization?
The agile approach says that all the employees act on the same level and as teams. Without specifications and objectives of the Top Management. Controlling themselves and self-managing. The team consists of different employees, who work in a specific, previously defined department/area. However, and this is the important difference, without a leader. Similarly without specifications from the top management in the form of „100 pieces per hour to be reached" or other specifications. The Team itself decides and indeed sets itself objectives, which however the team wants to achieve. Similarly, the team determines the organizational points, as for instance, who works at which workplace, who may/can go on a holiday, etc. Topics like further

development of the individual processes within the department are also a part of self-control, like which training, and schooling are necessary at which workplace. Also, in the investment subjects the team, in agreement with the Top Management, is clearly having the responsibility, as also regarding the subject of financial success. The objectives are worked out and set within the team. Then the self-set objectives are also attempted to be achieved as self-set objectives. And there the psychology is massively used. A self-controlled team, which sets objectives for itself, develops a self-running compulsion not only to reach the objectives but also to be better and better. That is to improve oneself continuously. Self-determination makes this possible. The discussions, as to which objectives must be reached, are not carried out by managers and management requirements. These are rather the own ideas, which should alleviate the need at the workplace. The need could be the points like un-planned standstills and errors, which occur during the shift, or during the work period and thus endanger the self-planned objectives. It certainly lasts for a time span, till this machinery begins to run, however, if the internal urge to succeed, which always motivates more and more to reach the objectives, and which the team itself has imposed upon itself, so strong, that it mutates to automatism. It is the same effect as during a game. Here due to the internal urge everything is set on reaching the next level or to achieve new records.

Naturally the team pushes its boundaries, when for instance imparting knowledge or differences of opinion within the team are involved. For this purpose, there is a coach, who is available to the individual teams. This is not a manager, moreover an advisor and companion, who advises the team from the outside and coaches. A coach has several teams, which he looks after and accompanies. The coach serves as conveyor of knowledge and as mediator, when it is necessary to promote further development of the team or to arbitrate in case of disagreement. The coach also acts, if it is necessary, as arbitrator between the team members. His main function is however to give thought impetuses and knowledge. So that the team members do not swim in their own confusion of thoughts in a circle and step on the stand on the subject of further development.

A revolutionary approach? Yes, certainly, however an approach, which is rewarding when it passes through the head and tested in a pilot test. Self-decision is the highest form of integration of all employees and only when all the employees are integrated and pull on one string, the results shall be more efficient and effective or come more sustained, since the „ownership" behavior becomes apparent very quickly and influences the decisions.

Premium models are also a good factor to increase the motivation within the team. Also, in agile approach recognition and appreciation are important factors. Since there are no specifications or target specifications from the side of the top management, there can for instance be a premium scheme, that every time when a production record of OK products is reached, there is a premium payment to the extent of x €. At the beginning there shall certainly be more premia (number of premia) paid. However, coupled with a productivity index, at the beginning smaller amounts shall be paid. With increasing rise of the productivity, it shall be more difficult to reach new production records. The curve shall be flatter, however, every increase in the productivity then operates a greater lever of economy. Through the coupling with a productivity key figure, the number of premiums shall be lower, however the level of premiums increases. Thus, also here the motivation for reaching new objectives still remains as incentive in addition to the self-determination in the team.

The importance lies in the placement of functions and in the clear understanding of the team with respect to the new organization. The equality rule and the acting without superiors, which continuously tells what OK is or what is not OK, or what who when has to carry out, is essential. In the agile model all the team members are asked to take the decisions in collective and to separate oneself from the thought that one gives the command and that only he has responsibility.

The pay system is also constructed uniformly. Each team member receives the same pay, independently of the affiliation. Thus all the tensions of the „jealousy" thought are gone. In case of this model the team concept is extremely strongly promoted. The team notices very quickly that if not all members make their contribution, there are no successes to celebrate.

The size of the individual team consists of up to 9 persons. Beyond this the self-determination does not function anymore, since there are too many discussions and it would lead to the formation of different groups within the team.

What happens thus, when a fabrication line requires more than 9 persons in order to manufacture products?

Then 2 or more teams shall be implemented. However, the risk exists in the fact that in a chain production there can be tensions between the teams. The reason for this is in the fact that one team works perhaps more efficiently than the other and thus is braked. Here it is necessary to work out a common objective through the coach and to represent clearly a customer/supplier relationship. Similarly, it must be conveyed to the individual teams that the problems of the supplier are the problems of the customer. The objective is to implement a „supporting" team culture, which jointly takes up the superior problems and turns them off consistently or sustainably. For this purpose, the Commitment/ approval of all is necessary to follow this path.

- Which important differences are there between the agile and the team-oriented form of organization?

- Which advantages does the agile form of organization have vis-à-vis other forms of organization?

- What is achieved with the agile organization structure?

- Which pre-requisites must be created for an agile organization form?

- How an agile organization structure is created?

Commitment of the entire team, however, even more from the Top Management is basic pre-requisite to implement a change. This is valid not only for changes, however, it has here the greatest negative, as also positive effect.

In other words, to live or to show the new strategy, the new way. Authentically and comprehensibly transparent, so that everyone in the organization can feel that this is the way, which is used or followed in this organization. Especially in change or modification processes not all employees shall be immediately ready to accompany on the new way. Change includes also fears and doubts, which release safety thoughts in different manifestations in the individual employees. These fears and doubts or uncertainty can be counteracted strongly with information and accompaniment. A „WIN WIN" situation must be created that creates or produces an environment for the employees, which enables motivation. Basically, most of the employees want to traverse the path of the management, however, they also do not want to fail or be overwhelmed. Not to lose that, what they have perhaps created for themselves over the years or to fail in new things, perhaps not come along in case of new areas. In part, employees have the fear to lose their face in front of the new, younger colleagues and especially not immediately to master new technologies. Especially when new technologies are involved, it is necessary to let the old and long serving employees to have support. New plants and machines must be learnt. The employee controlled the „old" workplace, not the new one. He must learn this, perhaps starting from zero. Not easy for the long-serving employee. It should be considered to offer such long-serving, very experienced and knowledgeable employees the possibility to convey their knowledge to other employees. Especially their product knowledge is of great significance. As trainer in the worker development program the employee, on the one hand, can convey his experience and his knowledge and on the other hand, lifts himself up a little from the new employees and has less fear of contact, if it involves learning or accepting something new

It is another failure recipe, when the top management does not stand authentically and transparently behind the change, i.e. behind the worker development program. Without this commitment there is no possibility implementing the program durably in the organization and to use it successfully.

- What must be procured for the employees so that the organization acts successfully?

- How a commitment/ approval is achieved within the team?

- What is the function of the management in the promotion of the commitment within the team?

The training of the individual knowledge levels is considered for all employees. However, there shall perhaps be employees, who fear changes more and see them with more skepticism than others. Other employees shall perhaps defend themselves against starting a training course. Different reasons can act against this decisively.

- Fear of the new
- Fear that training exceeds the capabilities
- Fear of examination
- Fear of change
- Discomfort at the thought as employee working over several years now having to press the "school bench" simultaneously with the new employee
- Fear to lose the own, built position in the undertaking (to have to surrender the castle, since everyone can obtain the knowledge and one's own knowledge is not so exclusive anymore)
- etc.

These fears and worries can be counteracted to a great extent with clarification and by active communication. Although there shall be many, who shall openly approach the training, there shall be other employees, who are less ready to take this step.

Therefore, it is important that employees report themselves on their own for this program or can report. It is also a possibility to carry out intensive enlightenment talks with the „old established" employees, so that they can be convinced with arguments to go along. There is a possibility to train exactly these employees as the first ones. With that these ones would have on the one hand a start over the other new employees, and on the other hand, they would not form a barrier or counter front. As against this the employees, who were or are taken up anew, shall have the possibility to begin the intensive training program, only after the end of the trial period.

Service seniority

The employee must have completed the trial period successfully so that participation is possible. Reaching of knowledge level BASIS Level 1, Beginner (Learning phase) is pre-requisite for every function.

Own Interest

The employee himself must be interested in his personal training and advanced training and shows the readiness to go the „Extra mile" and to make the extra effort.

Potential

From the observation and evaluation of the employee the manager must give a recommendation, whether and when the employee should be promoted in the Worker Development Program.

Decision

With the help of factual, comprehensible and transparent criteria in the individual areas like requirement, potential and capability of the employee as well as the number of possible candidates it is decided as to who and when promotion is given in the program.

Registration

The employee is registered for the further development for the Worker Development Program, briefly ODP, and a corresponding PDP, also called IDP, (personal development plan) is prepared.

Schooling / Training

The employee is trained on the corresponding module and prepared for the certification (the employee must pass a knowledge test).

Further Steps

With the help of an employee interview with the employee, as also according to the current requirement it is decided, whether and if yes, which track the employee shall follow. Depending upon the decision the PDP/IDP shall be continued -> Generalist, Specialist/Expert or manager (Team leader)

Further schooling / training

The employee is trained on the corresponding next module and prepared for the certification (the employee must pass a knowledge testing).

Re- Certification

Every year a re-certification is carried out with the employee. During this all criteria in his knowledge level should be fulfilled. The factual result is recorded using his performance over the completed year and his knowledge level/ knowledge in his training plan and it represents the ensuring of his pay according to knowledge level and area.

Employee discussion/ Feedback discussion

The employee receives feedback after every certification or re-certification through the trainers and his manager. The evaluation represents the basis of the yearly employee interview and flows in fully on material basis. Similarly, the next development steps are discussed, agreed upon and recorded in the personal development plan (PDP) in writing.

Efffect on wages / salary

The certification/re-certification flows, on the one hand, into the yearly employee interviews, and on the other hand the reaching or not reaching of a knowledge level also represents a possible change of the pay to the respective employee. With a successive re-certification the pay remains the same, as against this on not reaching the certification, the pay is matched correspondingly to the new knowledge level. This applies similarly on reaching a new, higher knowledge level, which in turn has a positive effect on the pay of the employee.

The advantage in this case is that all the employees know as to which monthly income is paid at which level. In a large number of units, the bandwidths are greatly scattered. Described in other words this means that for the same work different payments take place. The so-called official status, namely, to receive a better payment due to age, is really not a fair type of improved payment in comparison with other employees, who provide the same performance. However, one possibility is to implement a separate bonus agreement, which, after a staggering of 5, 10, 15, 20, etc. years in the company, is paid out to the employee in addition to the monthly salary. The uneven payment landscape of pays in a number of units is due to the grown structures, which have risen within the organization in the course of years. Also, the personal aspects of many managers to pay the employees better, who show up more, as also to give preferential treatment to those employees, who face more often, was the order of the day, even though there are only a few, who would confess this. In order to bring this subject on an objective, fair and transparent level, the

Worker Development Program suits very well. It is up to the employee himself to engage himself and to develop himself further continuously. Thus, the employees themselves have it in their hand, as to how the payment looks and how the employees can reach the respective development stage. In the team-oriented organization structure the managers as well as the employees themselves are responsible for the further development.

In an agile form of organization, the employees themselves are required to develop themselves further in order to reach their own objectives, however, the role of the advisor/companion is also an important one with arguments and explanations to convince the employees to go along the path of the CIPs or juxtapose the external picture of the employee with the internal one and to show up critically.

- Which importance should the training assume in an undertaking?

- During changes in the organization what should receive special attention?

- Why is a certification necessary?

- What does the re-certification serve for?

- How does the worker development program affect the payment structures in the organization?

There are again and again good discussions, whether internal trainers are better, more efficient and cost-wise more favorable than external trainers. External trainers have the reputation to be cost intensive, however more thorough, who bring in new ideas and knowledge from other undertakings or projects.
Therefore, and against are manifold and could be stated endlessly.

The internal as well as the external trainers have their justification. They should be selected only very carefully with reference to the respective situation and function. A good mix between the two ensures success in the Worker Development Program. Only which topics should be awarded/ allocated to the internal or external trainer? This depends upon the organization and its competences in the area's knowledge and knowledge management. Should there be an own department for organization development with internal trainers, then the access to external trainers shall reduce noticeably. Although, it is always good not to swim to 100% in one's own „knowledge soup". External trainers bring other views and representations, which can be very fruitful in one or the other case. However, the pre-requisite is that it was aligned oriented on the desired structure of the undertaking and attuned with the client in the background. A not attuned procedure can very much start „backwards", i.e. can release very counter-productive effects within the organization and bring a lot of unrest in to the team.

A certification is not always popular among the employees. Merely the thought of an examination, as in school, releases a feeling of being unwell in many people. The reason for this is probably to be found in the fear of failure. A certification is a scrutiny of knowledge; however, it is necessary to ensure the transfer of knowledge.

A certification is carried out for each knowledge level. It is the conclusion of a training, or of the annual review, which has an influence on the payment to the individual employees.

A knowledge scrutiny (certification) is similarly a basis for the annual employee interview, as also a confirmation of the performance of the employee on a very factual basis.

Thus, the evaluation of the respective employee is carried out in different areas during the certification process.

The areas are the following:

- Theory
- Practice
- Daily work at the workplace

In the theoretical review the contents of the individual classroom trainings are questioned with respect to understanding. It is important for the success, that the theory was understood by the individual employees. What was not understood in the theory, shall function with great difficulty in the practice.

During the practice scrutiny individual work processes are played and thus the application is checked. For example, work safety processes are demonstrated for the scrutiny of safety devices, quality assurance processes for ensuring the product quality or setting changes or tool changing processes by the respective employee. These are checked and evaluated by an expert.

Under the point daily activity at the workplace are the daily work processes, which stand in focus. In order that no snapshots come for evaluation, regular controls are carried out at the workplace.

Among other things the following is controlled:

- Is the work environment controlled for work safety at the beginning of the shift
- Is the workplace clean
- Were all cleanings and inspections implemented according the TPM (total productive maintenance / preventive maintenance) Plan and entered in the Check List
- Is the OEE (Total Plant Efficiency) List exactly maintained
- Are the quality checks carried out according to specifications?
- Does the employee work according to his handbook and does he carry it with him?
- etc.

It is the daily mode of working which should be fairly and transparently checked here. Work processes as for example scrutiny of the safety devices at the beginning of the shift does not serve only for fulfilling the specifications.

The scrutiny of safety technical devices or the scrutiny of sources of risk serves much rather the safety of the employee or the employees, who work in this work environment. It should be the first priority for every undertaking that the entrusted employees go home as healthy, as they have come to work. These are mainly facilities like work surroundings or machines or tools and modes of operation, however, there is the much-underestimated stress factor, which stresses the employees more or less. However, one thing can be said clearly:

„Standardized workplaces and a clear regulation of roles and responsibilities are the basic prerequisites, to solve the upcoming problems and targets objectively and transparently. Provided however, with the full support of the entire management team! "

In summary the following can be said:

A certification serves for the scrutiny of knowledge and mode of working of the respective employee. After every certification, in the next knowledge level the employee comes to enjoy a knowledge allowance, which shall be a part of his payment up to the knowledge scrutiny / certification taking place yearly.
Through the compliance of the SOSs and the consequent implementation of individual functions, the workplace shall be more secure, productive and thus more stress-free. Thus, one has to proceed from the assumption that

the employee finds a motivating work environment after his training phase. Also, this is employee binding and demands a corresponding culture of the undertaking.

In total there are 4 knowledge levels, whereby the fourth knowledge level represents a trainer or instructor level.

All the training programs in the individual knowledge levels are clearly divided and show the same structure.

There are respectively the same training parts:

- Theory training in the „class room"
- Practical training at the workplace or, if available at a learning place (for example a trainee welding station)
- Mode of working – „learning by doing" at the respective workplace with and without supervision (depending upon the knowledge level)
- Dealing with colleagues and managers

Knowledge level BASIS

Serves his work area with small troubleshooting assignments, at the beginning with support and in useful period independently.

Possesses solid basic knowledge about work area, simple maintenance jobs as well as the relevant basic criteria like product quality, work safety and environment.

Knowledge area EXPANDED

Employee can service his work area independently, clean and carry out maintenance jobs. He reacts confidently in case of faults and knows what is to be done. He possesses deep knowledge in the work area inclusive of the relevant basic criteria like product quality, work safety and environment. He brings in improvement potentials actively.

Knowledge area EXPERT

He has high and detailed specialist knowledge in the work area as also the required knowledge about the relevant basic criteria like product quality, work safety and environment and brings in improvement potentials actively and can also process these independently.

COMPETENCE AREA TRAINER

He is expert and has the capability to give further/convey knowledge.

For the overall representation of the periodic sequence the following graphic should give a clear overview.

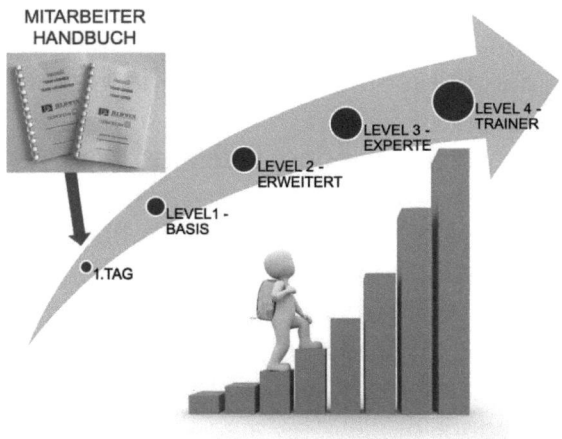

EMPLOYEE HANDBOOK

1st	Level1	Level2		Level3	Level4

Day BASIC EXTENDED EXPERT TRAINER

The first knowledge level is the basic knowledge level. Every employee undergoes the training of the basic knowledge. There is a time limit, which the employee should not exceed during his training, before he is certified.

For the basic knowledge level, as also for every other knowledge level, several parts of a specified training program are to be completed as described above.

In summary this involves getting acquainted with the work environment, the workplace in detail in the subjects of work safety and securing the product quality, as also the switching on and off of the machine/plant, so far as they are there. Always with guidance by the appointed trainer.

How long this time frame lasts, depends upon the respective organization and complexity of the workplaces.

An example, which is however dependent upon the organization and the industry, should be mentioned here.

In a metal processing industry with automated and semiautomatic plants and machines the training for basic knowledge lasts over 6 months. In this period the employee must have acquired the basic knowledge or must have successfully completed the certification / knowledge test.

The second knowledge level is the „extended knowledge level ". In this phase of the training, which all employees must do within a specified period, the knowledge of the first knowledge level is widened or extended.

Going through the individual knowledge levels within a predetermined period is necessary in order to determine fairly, whether the respective employee is used at the right working place. Every employee has competences/capabilities and interests in different manifestations. This is neither bad nor good. However, it is of significant importance for the success of the organization. If an employee is deployed in the „wrong" position, which the employee cannot fulfill, since he does not show any own interest or since the workplace exceeds his capabilities, then there is quickly overload for and frustration of the employee.

This helps neither the undertaking, nor can the employee stand this for long. The employee shall either leave the undertaking after some time, slide in to a „burn out ", or carry out his work frustrated and de-motivated.

That this is not target-oriented, efficient and conducive for the continuous improvement concept need not be mentioned here anymore. The probability of increased illnesses and poor mood-making in the undertaking is very high. Therefore, it is better to give the employee a possibility to expand his competences, however, also to the undertaking to evaluate the employee fairly and to deploy him there, where he feels well, as also to get the performance, which is expected from the respective employee.

If the employee is overwhelmed with the function or does not fit in the undertaking, then at a particular spot the proverbial „tearing leash" must be pulled, before a damage is caused in the employee in the form of sickness, and damage in the form of losses for the undertaking.

The third knowledge level is the Expert level. This is not provided for all the employees. Following the career path, there is a flexible or broad orientation, namely the expert orientation, which goes very much into the knowledge depth of the individual processes. During this not the diversity of the individual production processes is in focus. The important thing here is to train the employees, who get acquainted with the process in its total complexity and learn to understand or master it. The objective of this training is to find a contact partner for the daily technical and process-related concerns, which cannot be implemented/solved, to understand them and to find a solution for them. The further development on the process for more safety, more quality and productivity with the clear objective to reduce the costs sensibly is similarly in his area of responsibility.

One thing in advance and this must also be clearly communicated within the organization:

„In an organization there cannot be only experts and all other orientations in the undertaking are also important and equal like the one for experts! "

The philosophy of the „Heroes of the Undertaking" should not be in the way in an organization. Experts are important, however without employees with a flexible and broad training the undertaking shall not survive. It is an organism, which requires all participating fractions, in order to ensure the survival and the success in the market.

An expert training takes its own time, and it is dependent upon the complexity of the process. Therefore, in this case individual training plans should be worked out for each work process. This work, as also the training programs of all other knowledge levels certainly demand a lot of time and resources, at the end of the day the effort pays back several times. Measured and provable in the topics work safety, quality, productivity, stocks and organization development with effect on the costs or the profit.

- Which knowledge levels are there?

- What is the purpose of certification?

- Why are the knowledge levels divided into different stages?

- On the level of the undertaking, on the career thread of the individual employees, on what attention should be paid?

- Which types of scrutiny are there during the certification?

- What advantage does the undertaking have through the individual knowledge levels?

The development of the training program of the individual knowledge levels is very elaborate. The compilation of the program determines the structure of the competences of the individual employees and thus the training program contributes substantially to the success or failure of the undertaking sustainably. Although the training program can be matched at any time, the organization must pay attention to the fact that every change brings unrest in the undertaking and the employees, who have already done the training earlier, must be retrained. Similarly, the administration of the individual forms and documents must be completed or matched subsequently. It is recommended, if at all, to implement this maximum once in the year.

However, generally the following is valid:

„Rather work somewhat longer on the planning than spending time with changing programs later and bringing unrest in the organization. "

In this book an example of a training program of the knowledge level Knowledge Level

BASIC is presented, with the help of a metal processing industry in sheet processing, however, with a little adjustment, this program can be used for other organizations also.

Summary:
Preparation for safe and quality-conscious operating of the machine/s and knowing the materials used

Duration:
9 days

Objective:
Worker knows basic safety precautions and quality standards in his work area

Practical training of this module <u>on the machine only with trainer</u>!

1.1	**S - EHS**
1.1.1	Machine layout
1.1.1.1	Presentation of the Machines/Plant parts
1.1.1.2	Media overview (Power supply, main switch, air supply, lubricants,…)
1.1	**S - EHS**
1.1.2	Safety equipment – PPE
1.1.2.1	Safety shoes

1.1.2.2	Safety goggles
1.1.2.3	Hand gloves (depending upon work area)
1.1.2.4	Ear protection
1.1.2.5	Warning vest
1.1.2.6	Dust protection masks
1.1.2.7	Cleaning, maintenance
1.1.2.8	Report when not present
1.1	**S - EHS**
1.1.3	Almost accident & accident report
1.1.3.1	What is almost accident
1.1.3.2	Form for almost accident
1.1.3.3	Corrective measures and responsibilities
1.1.3.4	Risk in default & introduce countermeasures
1.1.3.5	Accident analysis of the almost accident
1.1.3.6	Data acquisition & processing
1.1	**S - EHS**
1.1.4	Chemicals
1.1.4.1	Used chemicals and their deployment
1.1.4.2	Protective gear while handling chemicals
1.1.4.3	Storage and transport of chemicals

1.1.4.4	Safety data sheets
1.1.4.5	Eye shower, safety shower
1.1.4.6	Safety equipment
1.1	**S - EHS**
1.1.5	Safety equipment
1.1.5.1	Protective doors
1.1.5.2	Emergency exit
1.1.5.3	Safety light barriers
1.1.5.4	Working at height
1.1.5.5	Working in narrow spaces
1.1.5.6	Check of alarms and protective devices
1.1	**S - EHS**
1.1.6	EMERGENCY-EXIT-Function
1.1.6.1	Check for functioning (+ Documentation & Protocols)
1.1.6.2	Where are the emergency off switches
1.1.6.3	When is the emergency off switch required
1.1.6.4	Accessibility of the emergency off switches
1.1	**S - EHS**
1.1.7	Floor markings
1.1.7.1	Pedestrians use only marked walking paths
1.1.7.2	Blocked areas must remain free

1.1.7.3	Emergency exits must remain free
1.1.7.4	Colored markings (blue, red, green, yellow-black,…) and their meaning
1.1.7.5	Flight paths and walking paths in the area

1.2	**Q - QUALITY**
1.2.1	Test site
1.2.1.1	Cleanness at test site
1.2.1.2	Functions of the testing and measuring devices
1.2.1.3	Measuring units

1.2	**Q – QUALITY**
1.2.3	Measuring, documenting & reporting
1.2.3.1	Behavior in case of deviations
1.2.3.2	Explain test protocol
1.2.3.3	Data collection

1.3	**D-DELIVERY/PRODUCTIVITY**
1.3.1	Materials
1.3.1.1	Used materials (Handling and correct dealing with materials)
1.3.1.2	Products (End product)

Training list:
Knowledge level BASIC – Module 1

- PPE (personal protective equipment)
- Safety training
- Behavior in emergency
- Floor marking
- Almost accident & Accident report
- Protective gear for chemicals
- Safety facilities
- Emergency exit & Function
- Test site
- Measuring, documenting & reporting
- Materials
- Escalation process
- SOS / WES (standardized working sheet)
- Waste separation
- Product & packing training
- Behavior in Q-deviation / Containment

Practice-Test:

- Showing and explanation of work area, protective devices, Chemical containers, floor markings and raw material stores/delivery stores in the area
- Delimiting the work area
- Quality checks of the product and naming the fault types

- Explaining of used documents
- Naming of important machine components
- Knowing the escalation process
- Knowing the characteristics of raw materials

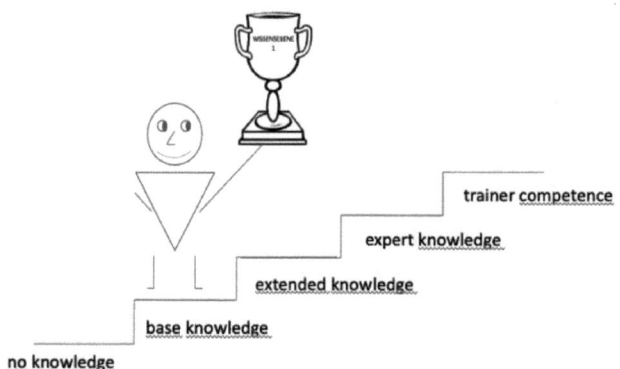

Summary:

Getting to know the theoretical and practical methods, in order to ensure a clean and orderly workplace, to minimize disturbances and to document these

Duration:

2 Weeks

Objective:

Worker knows specifications for the cleaning of his work area, recognizes the faults that appear, can document these and partly explain them

Practical training of this module on the machine only with supervision!

2.1	**Q - QUALITY**
2.1.1	Cleaning of workplace and surroundings
2.1.1.1	Right cleaning material for particular area
2.1.1.2	Shadow-Wall (Shadow board)
2.1.1.3	Work area Layout

2.1	**Q - QUALITY**
2.1.2	Cleaning -SOS´s
2.1.2.1	Understand SOS´s
2.1.2.2	Implementation of the SOS´s
2.1.2.3	Inspection of the SOS´s

2.1	**Q - QUALITY**
2.1.3	Cleaning Checklists
2.1.3.1	Understand Checklists
2.1.3.2	Implementation of Checklists
2.1.3.3	Inspection of Checklists

2.1	**Q - QUALITY**
2.1.4	Cleaning materials
2.1.4.1	Storage
2.1.4.2	Completeness / Inspection of cleaning
2.1.4.3	Functionality
2.1.4.4	Safe handling of cleaning agents
2.1.4.5	Consequences of defective cleaning

2.1	**Q - QUALITY**
2.1.5	Inspection of cleaning
2.1.5.1	Right cleaning tools
2.1.5.2	Right cleaning agents
2.1.5.3	Adhere to specifications
2.1.5.4	Inspect cleaning lists
2.1.5.5	Cleaning lists documentation

2.2	**DELIVERY/PRODUCTIVITY**
2.2.1	Maintain OEE-Lists (Disturbance documentation)
2.2.1.1	Exact disturbance periods
2.2.1.2	Detailed explanation of the disturbance
2.2.1.3	Changeover Periods
2.2.1.4	Complete filling and readability of the OEE Lists
2.2.1.5	Objective and use of OEE-Lists
2.2	**D - DELIVERY / PRODUCTIVITY**
2.2.2	Refill of raw materials/ components
2.2.2.1	BOM (Part list)
2.2.2.2	Filling of Checklists
2.2.2.3	Dealing with raw materials/ components
2.2.2.4	Specifications of raw materials
2.2	**D - DELIVERY / PRODUCTIVITY**
2.2.3	Functioning, process and technical condition of the machine
2.2.3.1	Main purpose of the machine
2.2.3.2	Explain process from-to (process explanation)
2.2.3.3	Risks of the machine & plant

2.2.3.4   Documentation
2.2.3.5   Escalation process
2.2.3.6   Conspicuous matters

Training list:
Knowledge level BASIC – Module 2

- Cleaning at workplace
- Cleaning & Inspection - SOS
- Cleaning- Checklists
- Cleaning materials
- Inspection & Cleaning
- Maintain OEE Lists
- Refill of raw materials
- Functionality, Process & technical condition of the machine / workplace
- 6S
- Evaluation & Pareto
- Electricals 1

Practical tests:

- Explaining of electrical switching elements on the machine
- Explaining of used checklists, documents and BOM
- Can carry out refill procedure of consumable materials

trainer competence

expert knowledge

extended knowledge

base knowledge

no knowledge

Summary:
Knowing operating/indicator elements, used materials and proper response in case of faults

Duration:
2 Weeks

Objective:
Worker can independently operate the machine/workplace, service it, rebuild it, remove simple disturbances and limit faults

Practical training of this module on the machine only with supervision!

3.1	**D - DELIVERY / PRODUCTIVITY**
3.1.1	Take Out
3.1.1.1	Understanding of Take Out (Weekend operation)
3.1.1.2	Disorder code
3.1.1.3	Remove raw materials from the machines (Excess)
3.1.1.4	Operate in basic position
3.1.1.5	Stop media (air etc.) supply

| 3.1.1.6 | Switch off current, main switch (of present) |
| 3.1.1.7 | Install safety lock |

3.1	**D - DELIVERY / PRODUCTIV-ITY**
3.1.2	Lock Out
3.1.2.1	Understanding of Lock Out
3.1.2.2	Disorder code
3.1.2.3	Remove raw materials from the machines (excess)
3.1.2.4	Operate in basic position
3.1.2.5	Stop air supply
3.1.2.6	Stop power supply, switch off main switch (if present)

3.1	**D - DELIVERY / PRODUCTIV-ITY**
3.1.3	Switch on/off & Start / Stop
3.1.3.1	Main switch - Functioning
3.1.3.2	Control voltage in screens (if present)
3.1.3.3	Container lock (pressure container) open/closed
3.1.3.4	Cross reference to media (air, Water, Lubrication,…)

| 3.1 | **D - DELIVERY / PRODUCTIV-ITY** |
| 3.1.4 | Operating/Indicator elements |

3.1.4.1	Correct applications
3.1.4.2	Functions
3.1.4.3	Speed settings (feed etc.)

3.1	**D - DELIVERY / PRODUCTIV-ITY**
3.1.5	Operate basic position
3.1.5.1	What is the basic position (machine dependent)
3.1.5.2	For what the basic position is useful
3.1.5.3	Types of basic positions

3.1	**D - DELIVERY / PRODUCTIV-ITY**
3.1.6	Used media (fuels: air, electricity, hydraulics, gas,…)
3.1.6.1	Pay attention to leakages
3.1.6.2	Availability
3.1.6.3	Risk sources due to used media

3.1	**D - DELIVERY / PRODUCTIV-ITY**
3.1.7	Activate protective device (open/close protective grid) & properties
3.1.7.1	Before start of production check for function

| 3.1.7.2 | Explanation of the protective devices |
| 3.1.7.3 | Activity when manipulations are discovered (inform team leader or department head, stop the machines, etc.....) |

3.1	**D - DELIVERY / PRODUCTIVITY**
3.1.8	Carry out changeover
3.1.8.1	Inspection for available tools and re-fitting parts
3.1.8.2	Proceed step by step according to plan
3.1.8.3	Accurate working spares readjusting

3.1	**D - DELIVERY / PRODUCTIVITY**
3.1.9	Simple troubleshooting
3.1.9.1	Adjust the wrongly placed and dirty initiators
3.1.9.2	Adjust the guides
3.1.9.3	Adjust the transport bands/ lifts inlet/outlet (door lifts pneumatically)
3.1.9.4	Instruction to specific machines

| 3.2 | **Q - QUALITY** |
| 3.2.1 | Containment |

3.2.1.1	Procedure in case of quality deviations (right procedure, limiting the error, countermeasures)
3.2.1.2	Inform team leader/department head (Mail-distributor for stoppages)
3.2.1.3	Inform quality assurance QA
3.2.1.4	Problem solving
3.3	**S - EHS**
3.3.1	Waste separation & Waste management
3.3.1.1	ISO 14001 - Specifications
3.3.1.2	Indicate locations for waste containers per machine
3.3.1.3	Collection points
3.3.1.4	Outward transport

Training list:
Knowledge level BASIC – Module 3

- Take out
- Lock out
- Switch on and off of the Machine
- Operating and indicator elements
- Basic position for operating
- Used media (Fuels– air, electricity etc..)
- Activate protective device and behavior
- Changeover / Tool change/ Product change
- Simple fault removal
- Containment
- Waste separation & waste management
- 5 Why

Practical tests:

- Supply to the machine with media
- Basic position on & off, Start &Stop, Take Out
- Show and explain protective devices
- Carry out Change Over in specified time and quality
- Explaining of the operating/indicator elements & of machine components

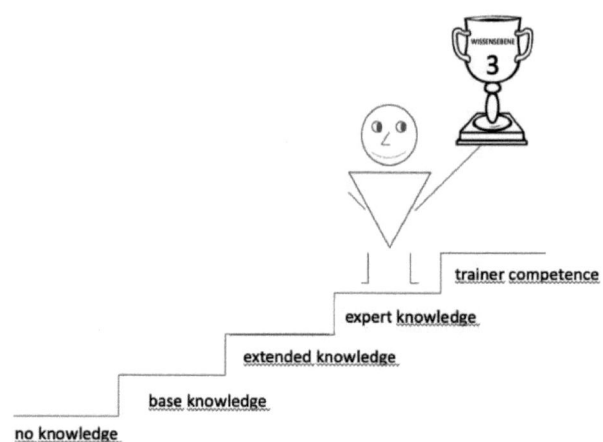

trainer competence

expert knowledge

extended knowledge

base knowledge

no knowledge

Summary:
Independent implementation and deepening the acquired knowledge and capabilities from methods and subject trainings

Duration:
2 Weeks

Objective:
Worker sees himself as team member, is capable (i.e. possesses knowledge and capabilities) to make his contribution and can operate the machine / workplace as Operator Level BASIC.

Practice portion of this module is carried out without supervision.

Practice:

- Collect experience through independent operating of the machine and implement what is learned.
- Develop understanding foer the production

- Cooperation during revision under guidance

Training list:
Knowledge level BASIC – Module 4

- 7 Types of waste
- Lean Part I
- Key figures (KPI)
- Lean Boards
- Shift handover
- Communication
- IS – System
- SIOs – recognize, document, process

Practice tests:

- Name important points for shift handover
- Explain individual key figures on TEAM Board / TIC (team info center)

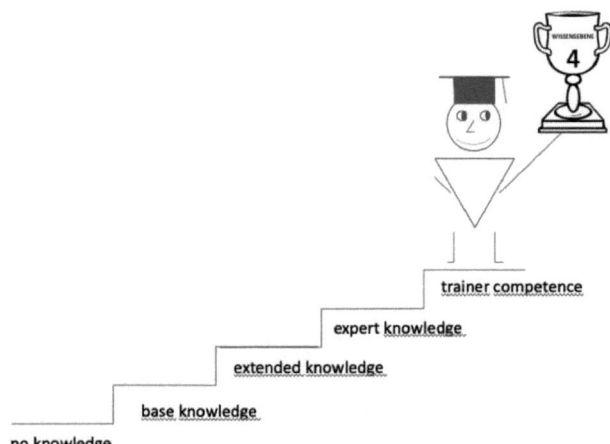

trainer competence

expert knowledge

extended knowledge

base knowledge

no knowledge

An essential advantage of the Worker Development Program is the factual payment possibility.

In many undertakings there is a non-transparent pay structure, which has grown in course of time. Limited possibility of comparison and partly a lot of displeasure in the team are the consequence, when the employees cannot understand why a colleague at the same workplace is paid better than he himself. Especially when he carries out the same functions and performance, however, works in the other shift.

With a transparent and comprehensible payment system these abuses, and the unrest can be removed.

The result would be a defined workplace, which includes a compensation x. Depending upon the stage of knowledge and the width of the knowledge, with reference to other workplaces, the employee can himself directly influence his compensation.

Thus a „WIN WIN" situation between the employee and the undertaking is created, which in turn supports the achievement of the objectives and thus the success of the undertaking.

This example serves for improved illustration and helps itself of fictitious payment sums, which must be adapted in the respective undertaking and to the respective laws.

Important here is the fact that the employee must reach the stages Basic and extended knowledge within a specified period. These 2 stages on at least one workplace are the fundamental requirement that the employee remains in the organization. In case of an employee, who does not reach the knowledge stage extended knowledge on at least one workplace, it is to be questioned, whether the employee fits in to the organization or is overwhelmed with the requirements and thus even from the employee side, in the middle and long term, it does not make any sense for him to remain in the undertaking. So hard as this may sound, there is also the responsibility of the employer vis-à-vis the employee. And when an employee is overwhelmed continuously, the employee perhaps lapses in to stress scenes, which, at the end of the day, perhaps lead to a „burn out", and no one can call this to be his objective, neither the employee nor the undertaking.

Here once again the knowledge stages, which an employee can achieve within the organization:

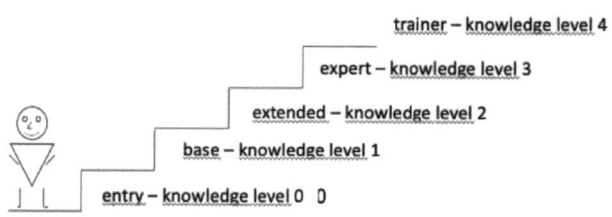

trainer – knowledge level 4

expert – knowledge level 3

extended – knowledge level 2

base – knowledge level 1

entry – knowledge level 0   0

The entry means knowledge level 0, since the employee cannot know the workplaces. After this follows the Basic Knowledge, whereby this step conveys a basic knowledge, however, with this knowledge the employee can service the workplace only limitedly. The objective is, that the employee reaches the knowledge level "extended knowledge" within a period specified by the organization, since in this case the employee generates a high utility value for the undertaking and thus can participate actively towards the success of the undertaking.

After the extended knowledge level there are two possibilities for the employee to develop himself further. Depending upon competence/capability of the employee and the requirement of the organization, the employee can decide either in the direction Expert, with the possibility to Trainer, or in the flexibility to be able to service several workplaces. All directions are to be seen as equivalent and they are equally important for the success of the undertaking.

	workplace 1	workplace 2	workplace 3	workplace x
	trainer	trainer	trainer	trainer
	expert	expert	expert	expert
	extended	extended	extended	extended
	base	base	base	base
	no knowledge	no knowledge	no knowledge	no knowledge

knowledge level

knowledge competence on workplaces

Just like the development of capability/extension of competence of the employee, the employee can positively influence his pay. The more flexible and deeper his knowledge progresses at one or several workplaces, the more positively his pay is affected, provided the employee retains his competence and demonstrates this in the annual re-certification.

A model should demonstrate this better.

knowledge level	workplace 1	workplace 2	workplace 3	workplace x
	+300 € / certificate			
	+100 €	+100 €	+100 €	+100 €
	1700 €	+100 €	+100 €	+100 €
	1600 €	+50 €	+50 €	+50 €
	1510 €			

knowledge competence on workplaces

In this fictitious example the remuneration levels and the possibilities are shown to influence the pay positively. A model, which is transparent and comprehensible, every employee can understand and thus also accept it.

knowledge level	workplace 1	workplace 2	workplace 3	workplace x
	+300 € / certificate			
	+100 €	+100 €	+100 €	+100 €
	1700 €	+100 €	+100 €	+100 €
	1600 €	+50 €	+50 €	+50 €
	1510 €			

knowledge competence on workplaces

During his recruitment the employee X has received a starting pay of 1500 Euro per month. During his successful certification at workplace I, he could demonstrate his BASIC

Knowledge and from the successful certification onwards he is paid 1600 Euro per month. Since the employee extended his knowledge within the time specified by the organization and reached the next knowledge level (extended knowledge) and also proved this in a successful certification, the employee is paid immediately with an improved remuneration level of 1700 Euro.

Now, the employee has the choice to direct his career in the direction Expert and Trainer or the direction Flexibility to build a broader knowledge. Naturally these decisions are jointly made or agreed upon with the organization. It is important for the success of the employee and the undertaking to deploy the employees according to their capabilities and potentials. Therefore, a feedback conversation after every reached knowledge level or at least once in the year is a must. It is essential to match alien image with the self-image of the employee fairly and transparently.

In the example shown here the employee decides himself in agreement with the organization for making flexible his activities and the employee acquires the Basic Knowledge, the extended knowledge of the Workplace II, as well as the Basic Knowledge of the Workplace III. Naturally in the predetermined period and in agreement with the organization.

After successful certification of the knowledge areas, the employee in this example has been able to improve his pay to 1900 Euro.

Through his success the employee has created himself an environment, which motivates him, and which shall lead to further successes.

The one-time reaching of a knowledge level and the receiving of the improved pay continues to persist only so long as the regular re-certifications are positively achieved. Should this not be the case, and the employee could not prove his knowledge at a workplace, then the additional pay is omitted. However, the employee has the possibility to achieve the lost knowledge level once again and thus to improve his raise once again. The objective of the Worker Development Program is not to bring the employee only once to a knowledge level, moreover, it is the objective to enable a continuous improvement of his knowledge level, of his competences and thus to continuously develop further also the organization, following the CIP Process (continuous improvement process).

Only a marginal remark: The employee has still another possibility to improve his pay. With the help of the suggestion system, in case this is available in the undertaking, the employee can introduce his profit-making ideas into the organization. If this idea is accepted and implemented, an award follows and the employee also receives an amount here, which is paid out either as recognition or from calculation of a saving.

- What advantage does the ODP (Operator Development Program) have in comparison with the payment to the employees?

- Which advantages result from the pay model for the undertaking?

- Which motivation does the employee have apart from the possibility of further development, when the employee is engaged in the ODP?

In the implementation phase, among other things, the following subjects are important, and they should not be neglected:

- Consistent processing of the individual measures and actions
- Scrutiny of the progress on a regular basis
- Procedure according to PDCA
- Implementation of a line of communication
- Implementation of an escalation process
- Feedback conversations with the individual project members /team members
- etc.

The consistent and timely processing of the individual actions and measures is decisive for the modification project. On the one hand to show that this development strategy is important for the undertaking and on the other hand to generate continuity and clarity within the organization. It would not be advantageous to undertake the implementation half-heartedly. The employees notice and know the difference between the alibi action and seriously meant implementation of important projects and changes. The management must show pro-actively and continuously that this program is the future, and no road can pass by it.

During start of the project it is very much recommended to carry out extensive Information programs and to mentally tune all the employees and to „fetch them". When the employees recognize the utility for the organization and for themselves, then employees shall also pull on one and the same string with the management. As already described in the chapter Commitment, this is essential to generate success.

Similarly, it is important to communicate regularly. In order to report the position of things the first certifications must also be prepared, so that even the last employee knows that something special is happening here. Everyone would like to play in a winning team. To use successes to get the last doubters on board is nothing bad.

A very important point is the escalation communication. The escalation process is significant with reference to the crisis management and when something goes really wrong, because in every project unforeseen things do happen, which must be brought in order. Here it is important to have established a clear communication and decision-making process, That something can and shall happen is relatively certain, and how the organization handles this is part of a different script. And during this the reaction period is one of the most important points, which need to be observed.

Since during the modification or implementation of the Worker Development Program people are always involved, the communication is one of the key factors in order to move a project forward or to let it fail. The method of feedback conversations can also bring about real wonders here. If the employees feel involved and in demand or picked up, then the speed of implementation accelerates by a multiple. In many projects this aspect comes too short and many project managers do not understand the world anymore, when there are delays and resistance within the team.

A further point is the mode of operation as per PDCA. The PDCA circle indeed comes from the quality control area, however it is often implemented in projects in order to represent the status of the individual measures and actions more transparently.

The PDCA Circle tracks a non-ending loop of improvement. A kind of positively directed spiral. P stands for PLAN, D for the implementation (DO), C for Check – Scrutiny and A stands for ACT – to act.

Explained in other words, an action is planned, then implemented and measured, and when deviations to the objective are visible, countermeasures are introduced, and it begins once again from the beginning with the planning.

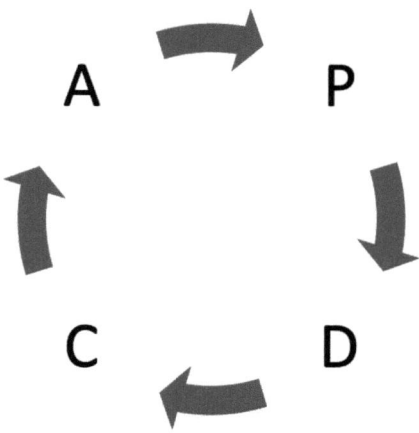

As already explained above, the failed recipes are a kind of cross-control from the negative point of view. In other words, all possibilities, as to why something does not function during a workshop, are worked out and listed by all the Workshop participants. In many instances thousands of reasons are named by employees, as to why something should not be changed, or why something shall not function. Thus, why not record all these arguments and objections and place the following question:

„What can we undertake that exactly these points do not occur? "

This question amazes most of the employees and as a rule during follow-up projects the arguments, which are mentioned against the occurrence, become more and more precise and generally formulated arguments are absent. The negative arguments, which in turn are kept more defined and not general, continue to prevail in many instances. And do not misunderstand, the „doubters" and „negative thinkers" are important in order to consider mindsets and possibilities in the foreground, which can cause problems during the implementation. However, too many are not so sparkling, when the implementation is involved.

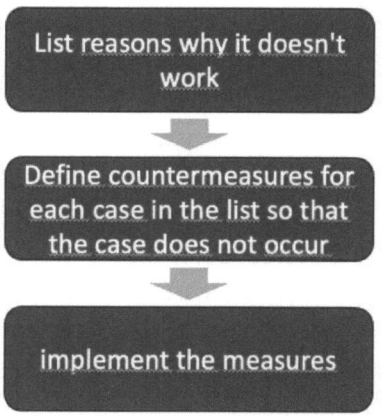

Reviews or also called scrutiny are a part of the everyday project life. Without checking, as to where does the project stand in the individual points, it shall be difficult to hold the course and the speed, which is necessary to implement the project successfully.

A communication board on the shopfloor is to be recommended, where all the employees at all times have the possibility to receive current information about the project. And the key to success lies in the topicality. Many information boards are not experienced. Many of these boards were created at the start for presentation to the Top Management or for some visitors and were never again updated. Such „dead" boards are information corpses. The view of the employees is a clear and simple one. No importance in the project is attributed to the boards with information, therefore, I as employee must also no more be interested in them. Because when the information and presentation table is not worth it to be updated and up to date, the project is also not important.

Less effort, however, a lot of effect in the team. Attention should be paid to the fact that the employees are repeatedly invited for information programs, experience new details in intranet, that internal social media report about the project, or perhaps something about it is reported in the employee newspaper. Then the importance is highlighted, because it is well-known to all within the organization.

As in almost any other project there are successes here. The first successes are the most important ones for the motivation of the individual employees. They show that it functions and that the project is profitable for the organization. As a rule, success motivates and inspires all participants. Therefore, it is important to honor these first successes and to celebrate them with the team. Thus, on the one hand in the team, and on the other hand in the remaining organization the successful start of the project is communicated.

Almost everyone wants to work with a „winning" team, to be part of the project and thus of the success.

This mood must be used for finding multiplicators for the project. The broader is the project communicated and carried continuously, the greater are the chances of success of the entire project. It is to be recommended to transport continuously the status and successfully concluded project sections into the organization in order to receive more acceptance and cooperation.

About one thing one can always be certain, that setbacks shall always be there. And this is good, because they remind us again and again that we are not all-knowing and infallible. And thus, we can always develop ourselves further. Reverses can also act in a motivating fashion and drive us to be still better, or to try it once again and to evaluate setbacks as an opportunity in order to realize an improved solution, which functions and can be implemented.

There are naturally situations, which do not exactly leave positive impressions on the mood of the team and on the motivation scale. However, if the team manages to overcome this deep, then it would return stronger from the situation and show that it is rewarding to traverse a path perhaps several times in order to reach the objective. However, it is important during this that the findings and experiences during failure are not forgotten. They should continuously remind us, as in a chess game, to consider a couple of steps forward and to implement a risk observation process. Risk management is an important part of every project and should be used really seriously.

In case of a few Worker Development Programs, which were implemented in organizations, it occurred that employees have realized their limits. This was realized through the fact that they for instance could not carry out the trainer function or could not reach the intended Expert level. Here it is important to „field" the employee and to oppose with explanations and understanding. It may indeed be a setback for the employee and for the organization, however it is a strength to know the weaknesses and limits and also to accept these, or in case of weaknesses at least to reduce these with countermeasures. However, should there be also employees, who find their limits in Level 1 or 2, then it may also be clearly inquired whether the work is the right one for the employee. It hardly brings something to the employee or to the undertaking, when employees work under stress in a workplace. There shall be increasing setbacks in the form qualitative or production-related matters and these cause frustration and costs, which in turn question the success of the undertaking. And this may also be a „banal" play of words, however, the weakest member of a chain forms the limit of resilience of the total organization. Therefore, the weakest member of the load limit should not be far too away from the remaining members.

ABBREVIATIONS

DESIGNATION	EXPLANATION
Teammember	employee production
ODP	operator development program
LDP	leader development program
Downtime	breakdown time of the machine / working place
PDP	personal development program
IDP	individuell developement program
CIP	continuous improvement process
TPM	total productive maintenance
OEE	overall efficiency equipment
PPE	personal protective equipment
SOS	standardized operating sheet
WES	working elements sheet
BOM	bill of material
QA	quality assurance

EHS	environment, health & safety
IS	improvement & suggestion system
SIO	safety information object
TIC	team info center
PDCA	Plan, Do, Check, Act

Further books by Marcus Karl HAMAN

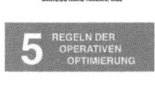

NOTES

NOTES

NOTES